Produced by GMC Publications Ltd.
86 High Street, Lewes, East Sussex, BN7 1XN, United Kingdom
www.thegmcgroup.com, +44 (0) 1273 477374

BEADED BALL NECKLACE

By Clair Wolfe

These beaded balls are incredibly easy and speedy to make and can be used in so many different ways. Use matching chain and beaded balls to make a fun and versatile necklace.

STEP 1

Cut a 12" length of thread and run through your hands to condition. Add four beads to the thread and pass along until about 3" from the end of the thread. Pass the needle back through the first bead added; pull the thread to form a circle of beads.

STEP 5

Add one bead and pass the needle through the bead furthest from the bead the working thread came out of. Add one more bead and pass the needle back through the bead the thread came out of.

MATERIALS

- FireLine® 6lb bead thread
- Size 12 beading needle
- Thread snips
- Selection of seed beads
- Length of aluminum chain
- Super glue
- Basic jewelry tools

STEP 2

Pass the needle through all beads once more to create rigidity. The working thread should be running the opposite way from the thread tail.

STEP 3

Add three beads to the thread and pass the needle back through the bead that the working thread came out of. Pass through the four beads once more before passing the needle through the first two of the three beads added.

STEP 4

Once again, add three beads to the thread and pass the needle back through the bead that the working thread came out of. Pass through the four beads once more before passing the needle through the first two of the three beads added.

PHOTOGRAPHS: LAUREL GUILFOYLE, CLAIR WOLFE

STEP 6

Pull the thread and create a circle of beads, as in Step 1. Pass the needle through all four beads a couple of times, making sure to keep the tension.

STEP 7

Turn the ball a quarter turn to the next four beads; pass the needle through a couple of times to secure into place, repeat around the ball until all the beads are securely stitched. This step is a little fiddly but gets easier the more balls you make.

STEP 8

Thread the needle through the beads until the working thread appears opposite the thread tail. Pull tightly, rolling the ball in your fingers to make sure all beads are sitting correctly. Use two surgeon's knots to secure, add a drop of glue to the knots and trim the excess thread.

STEP 9

Add a jumpring through opposite sides of the beaded ball and then add a length of chain to each side. Repeat until you have created a necklace of the desired length, finishing by adding a final beaded ball between two chain lengths and completing the necklace, no clasp is needed. Wear long, doubled or tripled over.

Extra Projects
Other ideas

MULTI-DANGLE PENDANT

Use jumprings to add the beaded balls to differing lengths of chain. Use another jumpring to attach the chains to a wire necklet, varying the height of the beads.

BRACELET

Use jumprings to attach a number of beaded balls to each other. Finish with short lengths of chain and a clasp.

MATERIALS

- 39" length of black leather cord
- Red magnetic clasp
- 30g packet of 3mm (size 8/0) black and red seed bead mix
- 0.3mm black coated wire
- Two-part adhesive

BUG BRACELET

By Tansy Wilson

The humble ladybug and butterfly clasp make up the theme for these beginners bracelets. Swap in any color of cord to match your favorite outfit.

STEP 1

Cut five lengths of black leather cord to suit your wrist measurement, approx. 7" each.

STEP 2

Mix up a small amount of two-part adhesive using a skewer and then put this glue into one end of your magnetic clasp. Ensure the glue is pushed all the way around the inside. Now one at a time push all your leather cords into this end, wipe away any excess glue and leave to dry.

STEP 3

Make a beaded ladybug following the bead pattern in the picture. Start at the bottom of the ladybug by threading the five beads onto 16" of black wire and work your way up to its head keep the tension as even as possible. Ensure the wire does not twist before you pull both ends at the same time. Leave the excess wire, as you will need it for Step 5.

PHOTOGRAPHS: LAUREL GUILFOYLE, TANSY WHEELER

STEP 4

Repeat Step 2 to glue the ends of the leather cord into the other side of the magnetic clasp. Once completely dry, find the center of three cords and bind them together using another small piece of black wire. Here make a pattern of the cords, forming a cross at the middle.

STEP 5

Place your beaded ladybug over the top of the bound wire at the center point and, using the excess lengths of wire left uncut from the head, sew the ladybug onto the leather cord.

STEP 6

When the ladybug is secure, cut away the excess lengths of wire. Use more lengths of black wire to join the leather cords together either side of the ladybug to keep the cross-shape intact.

Extra project Other ideas

You can also buy cute ladybug charms to add to leather cords using a jumpring. A different design on the same theme uses this butterfly clasp and keeps the leather cords all loose so the ladybug can move around.

FESTIVAL OF COLOR

By Tansy Wilson

Make this funky bracelet in wonderful bright colors to reflect the feel and flavor of a festival. These frosted glass beads are perfect to hold captured between the leather cord. This piece is really easy to make and perfect for a beginner.

MATERIALS

- 20" length of 6mm faux leather
- Strand of 8mm mixed colorful beads
- 50" length of embroidery floss
- Dressmaking needle
- Super glue

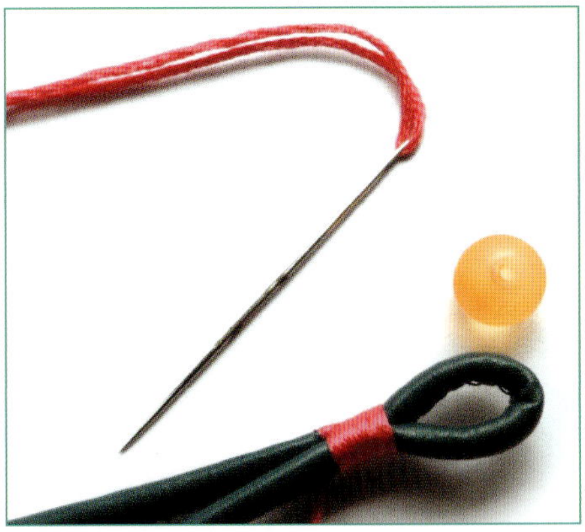

STEP 1

Thread a needle with a brightly colored contrasting embroidery floss. Fold the cord in half and form a loop just large enough to fit a bead through. Sew a few stitches at this point to secure the cord. Wrap the thread around the stitches to hide them.

STEP 2

Now continue to wrap the embroidery floss around each cord separately to form a figure eight pattern. Do this a few times, then, starting with the embroidery floss positioned at the top cord, take a bead and thread the needle through it and go down and around the bottom cord in the direction shown in the picture.

STEP 3

Thread the needle back through the same bead going the other way, and go over and around the top cord in the direction as shown in the picture. Pull the thread tight, securing the bead between the two cords.

PHOTOGRAPHS: LAUREL GUILFOYLE, TANSY WHEELER

STEP 4

Pick up another bead and thread the needle through it and down and around the bottom cord. Then go back through the bead and over and around the top cord. Keep repeating this step to add as many beads as appropriate for your wrist size. I used 16.

STEP 5

When you have added your last bead, wrap the embroidery floss around each separate cord to again create a figure eight pattern. Sew a few stitches to hold both cords in place.

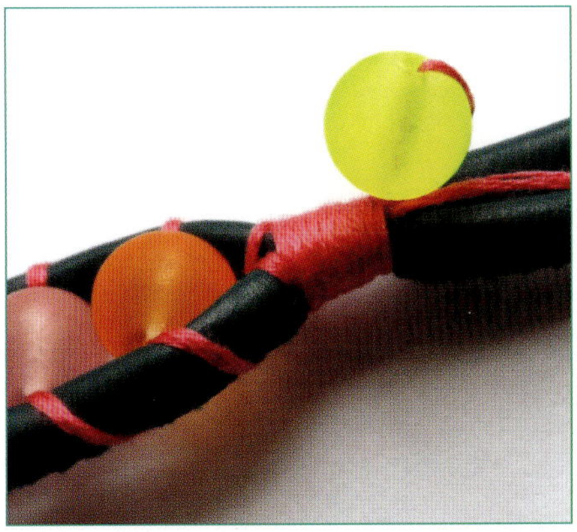

STEP 6

Finally, continue to wrap the embroidery floss around both cords to mirror the other end and then thread on another bead and sew another few stitches to secure it all in place. Cut away any excess cord and floss and add a few drops of super glue to secure.

Designer tips

- The first bead is always a bit tricky to position, but when you start repeating the beading process, it corrects itself.
- Try to keep the tension the same all the way through the bracelet so it remains straight. You may find it easier to work on a clipboard to hold it all in place. Work out what is the best method for you.

RED CORAL BEAUTY

By Tansy Wilson

Use bright red colored coral to make a statement with this fun necklace. Heart-shaped bead frames break up the coral beads.

MATERIALS

- Roll of nylon-coated jewelry beading wire
- Strand of red coral colored nugget beads
- 2 x heart-shaped bead frames
- Heart-shaped toggle clasp
- 2 x crimp tubes
- 2 x crimp covers
- Basic jewelry tools

STEP 1
A string of chunky natural cut gemstones or beads often come in assorted sizes. For this project, take all the beads off the string and sort as closely as possible into small, medium and large sizes. It doesn't have to be too exact.

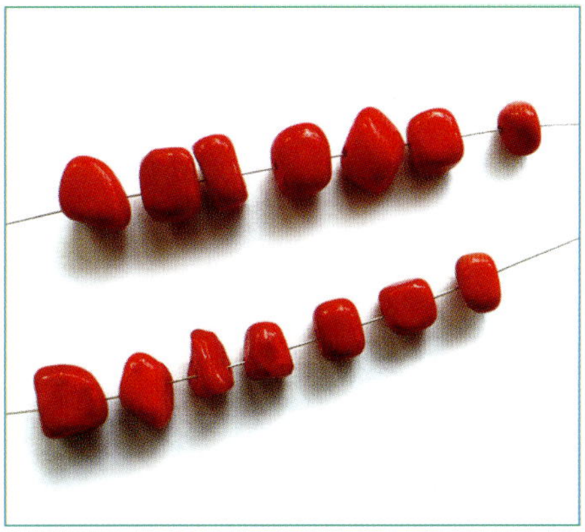

STEP 2
Cut two 24" lengths of nylon-coated wire and thread the following onto each one: four small, five medium and then seven large stones. Then add another five medium and four small stones the other side. Take one of the wires and add a further three small stones either side of this formation.

STEP 3
Lay the longer strung wire on the table and place the shorter strung wire above. Pass the ends of both wires from one side through the same hole on a heart-shaped bead frame. Repeat, passing both wires the other side through the holes of another heart-shaped bead frame.

PHOTOGRAPHS: LAUREL GUILFOYLE, TANSY WHEELER

STEP 4
Pull both wires at both ends tightly so the two bead filled wires gather together, hanging perfectly one under the other.

STEP 5
Now thread both wires through the same hole on the smaller sized beads to reach your desired length of necklace. I used 19 smallish beads on each side of each heart frame.

STEP 6
Finally, on one side, slide a crimp tube over both wires and thread both wires through the loop on a toggle clasp and back down through the tube. Pull the wire so the tube is snug against the clasp. Use crimping pliers and crimp the tube. Cut away excess wires and add a crimp cover. Repeat for the other side, attaching the toggle bar.

Extra project Make a bracelet

Make a matching bracelet by simply threading the beads on a single strand of nylon-coated wire, adding heart bead frames at regular intervals until you reach the desired length. Add a clasp using crimp tubes and covers following Step 6.

ALL IN BLUE

By Tansy Wilson

The beads used here are sodalite, which is a natural stone that bears a mottled resemblance to the deep blue of a stormy sea with cresting waves.

MATERIALS

- 40" length of blue suede with silver studs
- 5 x square blue sodalite beads
- 24 x 5mm round blue sodalite beads
- 24 silver ball headpins
- 2 x 10mm silver jumprings
- 2 x 4mm silver jumprings
- 2 x ribbon crimps
- Silver toggle clasp
- Nylon jewelry thread
- Super glue
- Basic jewelry tools

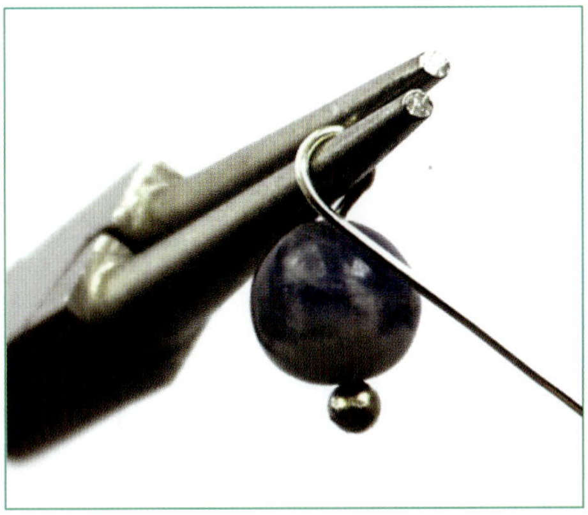

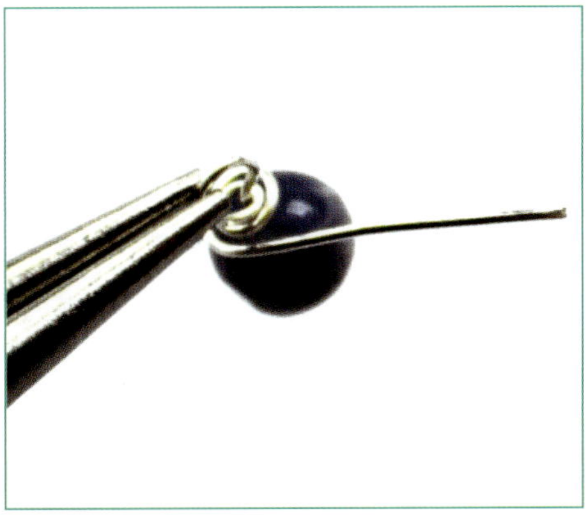

PHOTOGRAPHS: LAUREL GUILFOYLE, TANSY WHEELER

STEP 1

Thread a ball headpin through a 5mm bead and, holding it snugly to the bead, bend the long length of wire back against the bead. Hold the wire in the jaws of your round nose pliers so they are directly above the hole of the bead and bend the long length of the headpin around the jaws, forming a loop.

STEP 2

Remove your pliers and now use them to grip the back of the loop. Hold the long length of the headpin in your fingers and wrap it around the loop so it forms a spiral of wire on top of the bead. Cut away excess wire so you are left with a perfect wrapped loop. Repeat Steps 1 and 2 to make 24 wrapped loop beads.

STEP 3

Cut 20" of silver studded suede and fold it in half. Place the folded end just through a 10mm jumpring and then pass the cut ends through the loop of the fold. Pull both ends evenly so the suede secures itself onto the jumpring. Repeat this step with another 20" length of suede.

STEP 4

Cut 20" of nylon thread and thread one end through one of your 10mm jumprings. Pull the nylon so both ends are the same length. Pass both ends through the eye of a square stone bead.

STEP 5

Thread six of wrapped loop beads you made in Step 2 onto the nylon. Thread on another square bead. Keep alternating six beads then one square bead until you have used up all your beads and you have the two lengths of nylon coming out of a square bead. Thread both ends of nylon though the other 10mm jumpring and then back down through the square bead. Take one length and pass it through a wrapped loop and tie a secure knot. Add a drop of glue to knot.

STEP 6

Decide how long you would like your necklace to be and cut the studded suede pieces so they are the same length on either side. Place two lengths in a ribbon crimp, add a drop of glue and fold the crimp to trap and secure them in place. Repeat for the other side. Then add a toggle clasp using a 4mm jumpring at either end.

CLEVER CONNECTIONS

By Tansy Wilson

Use this simple way of making elasticated beaded links for a cleverly connected necklace, this would work just as well as a bracelet and could be made in your favorite colors.

MATERIALS

- 290 x 5mm glass beads (assorted colors)
- 2 x large curved tube bails
- 1 x large silver lobster clasp
- 8 3/4" length of silver large link curb chain
- Roll of elastic cord
- Super glue
- Basic jewelry tools

STEP 1

Thread 30 glass beads onto elastic and tie a knot so they all rest tightly together on the elastic loop. Add a drop of glue to the knot. Cut excess elastic away and slide the knot so it's hidden in the hole of a bead.

STEP 2

Repeat Step 1 so you make nine loops all with 30 beads each. I used different colors but you could have all the same or even use lots of different colored beads on the same loop.

STEP 3

Take one of your loops and squash it so it is long and thin, and then fold it in half.

PHOTOGRAPHS: LAUREL GUILFOYLE, TANSY WHEELER

STEP 4

I've secured this first loop of beads with an elastic band so I have both hands free. This makes it easier to take each beaded loop and fold it in half and pass it through the first beaded loop. Keep repeating this step until you have used all your beaded loops.

Designer tip

- Tying the elastic as tightly as possible ensures the beads are really close together to minimize exposed elastic.

STEP 5

Now you need to make end loops. Thread five beads onto another piece of elastic and then thread the elastic through a curved tube bail. Thread another five beads on the other side: don't tie a knot yet. Repeat this step to make another one.

STEP 6

Take one of your untied end loops and thread the elastic through the last folded loop. Pull the elastic as tight as possible and tie a knot, adding a drop of glue and cutting away excess ends. Open the end link on a length of large curb chain and link to the loop on the tube bail. Repeat for the other side and add a clasp in the middle to get your desired necklace length.

WESTERN SPARKLE

By Tansy Wilson

The main inspiration for these bracelets is diamanté, combined with the classic western cowboy boot. I found these boot charms and thought they fit the style perfectly and combined with leather-look cord it pays tribute to the western theme.

MATERIALS

- Cowboy boot charm
- 6mm by 4mm silver oval jumpring
- Fancy button
- 40" length of 1mm black leather-look cord
- 80" length of 0.8mm black leather-look cord or thick black beading thread
- 12" length of two-row diamanté trim
- Super glue
- Basic jewelry tools

STEP 1

Cut approximately 40" of 1mm black cord and thread a button onto it. Center the button on the length and then tie an 80" length of .8mm black cord as close to the left hand side of the button as possible. Add a drop of super glue to secure the knot and cut away excess short end.

STEP 2

Fold the 40" length of cord in half so the button is center top and the cord tied on is on the left. Use a clipboard and trap the button under the clamp. Stretch the two 20" lengths as taut as possible and clamp using a bulldog clip to the other end of the clipboard.

STEP 3

Cut 12" of diamanté strip and thread the 80" length of cord down through the central hole and under the right hand 20" length clamped to the board.

PHOTOGRAPHS: LAUREL GUILFOYLE, TANSY WHEELER

STEP 4

Then continue around the right hand cord coming over the top of it and thread back down through the same hole and then under the left hand clamped cord. Keep repeating the process of threading down through the next central hole along the diamanté strip and around the end cords.

STEP 5

When you have wrapped the entire length of diamanté you simply tie the cord you have been wrapping to one of the clamped end cords. Add a drop of super glue to secure and cut away any excess. Unclamp the end cords and tie a knot as close to the end of diamanté strip as possible. Then tie another knot, leaving a gap large enough to slide the button through.

STEP 6

You can tie another knot depending on how loose you want the bracelet to fit. Just check the button fits through. Then cut any excess end cords away. Open an oval silver jumpring and link through the cowboy boot charm and attach to the loop under the button.

LEOPARD PRINT

By Tansy Wilson

Beautiful leopard-print mother-of-pearl buttons, make this simple necklace really easy to make. Use the holes already drilled through the buttons to attach the individual pieces to a length of chain for a quick and stylish long necklace.

MATERIALS

- 30 x 11mm leopard-print buttons
- Black-colored heart clasp
- 2 x black-colored 4mm x 6mm oval jumprings
- 30 x antique silver-colored 5mm x 7mm oval jumprings
- 16" length of black-colored curb chain
- Basic jewelry tools

STEP 1
Cut your chain to 16" in length. Open a 4mm x 6mm oval jumpring and add on the clasp and attach to one end of the chain. Open another 4mm x 6mm oval jumpring and add the connector and attach to the other end of the chain.

STEP 2
Fold the chain in half and on the middle link of the chain add a 5mm x 7mm oval jumpring. Keep this jumpring open.

STEP 3
Take one of the leopard-print buttons and attach it to the open jumpring on the chain you added in Step 2 and close.

PHOTOGRAPHS: LAUREL GUILFOYLE, TANSY WHEELER

STEP 4
Add a jumpring to another button. Ensure the join of the jumpring is at the back of the button.

STEP 5
Link the next button on the chain to the left of the first button added in Step 3, leaving one link free. Now link another button to the left of the second button added in Step 3 again leaving a link free.

STEP 6
Continue adding buttons to the chain leaving a link free in between each one until you have used 15 buttons. Repeat, starting at center and adding buttons to the right. Double-check that the remaining empty lengths of chain are equal in length.

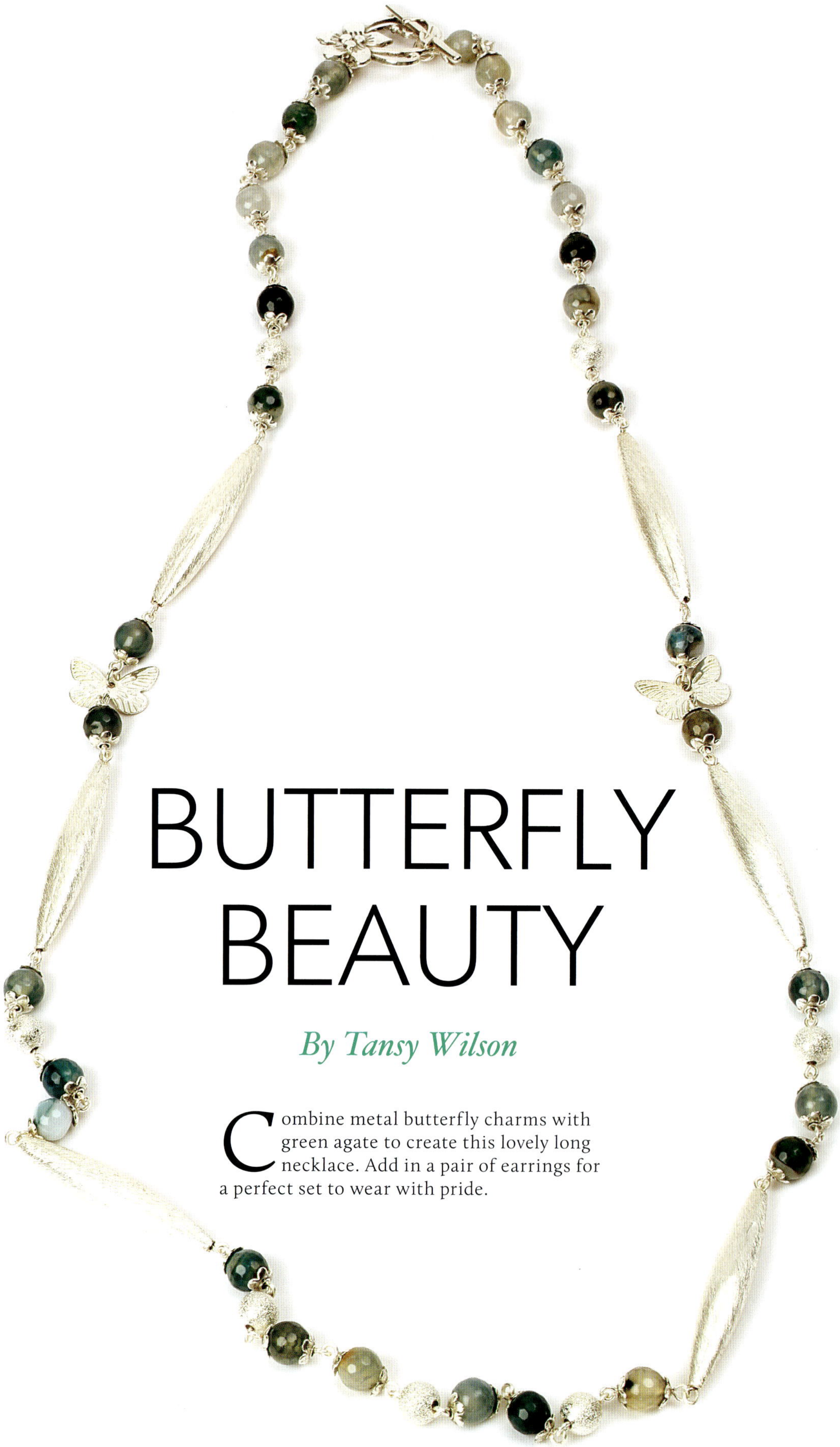

BUTTERFLY BEAUTY

By Tansy Wilson

Combine metal butterfly charms with green agate to create this lovely long necklace. Add in a pair of earrings for a perfect set to wear with pride.

Extra project Make earrings

Green agate beads usually come on a string so you should easily have enough to make matching earrings. Remember to keep two beads that are the same colour to make a matching pair.

MATERIALS

- 0.8mm (20 gauge) silver colored wire – to make your own eye pins
- 31 x green agate beads
- 7 x silver frosted beads
- 6 x 40mm silver bullet beads
- 62 x flower bead caps
- Decorative flower toggle clasp
- Basic jewelry tools

STEP 1

It is easier to make your own eye pins for this project, using 0.8mm wire. Cut approx. $1^1/_4$" of wire and make an eye loop at the very tip of the wire using round nose pliers. Thread your eye pin through a flower bead cap, followed by a green agate bead then finally through another flower cap.

STEP 2

Make another eye loop using round nose pliers as close to the top of the last added flower cap as possible. Cut away any excess wire.

STEP 3

Since you are making your own eye pins, you can make them the size you require to accommodate all your different sized beads. Repeat Steps 1 and 2 so you have all of your assorted beads ready to link together.

PHOTOGRAPHS: LAUREL GUILFOYLE, TANSY WHEELER

STEP 4

Open an oval jumpring and link through the top hole of a butterfly connector and close. Repeat, to add another oval jumpring to the bottom of the connector. Repeat this step to add jumprings to the other butterfly connector.

STEP 5

Arrange all your beads on a bead board playing around with ideas of symmetry or perhaps you would prefer a random pattern. Either way, when you are happy with your design, simply open one eye loop on a bead and link it to the next bead along.

STEP 6

The butterfly connectors will be linked by the jumprings added in Step 4. Keep working your way around the bead board ending up by joining a clasp using one jumpring either end.

CHA CHA

By Joan Gordon

Each link in this piece is handmade. You can also buy readymade findings, but once you make your own links and eye pins, you'll never go back to using premade findings.

MATERIALS

- 1" triangular mirror-backed crystal
- 12mm square mirror-backed crystal
- Shoe charm
- 2 x round donut shaped clasp ends
- 9" length of silver chain, parrot clasp and split ring
- 2 x $1\frac{1}{2}$" lengths of chain
- 6 x 4mm jumprings, one split ring
- 10 x 6mm jumprings
- 2 x 2cm wide silver motifs
- 2 x 6mm silver spacers
- Roll of 28 gauge wire for making eye pins
- Roll of 1mm round half-hard silver wire for making S-links
- 12 x $\frac{3}{8}$" long orange freshwater pearls
- 5 x 12mm wide glass beads
- Basic jewelry tools

Designer tips

- Be sure to store mirror-back crystals in a secure and protected case to avoid scratching.
- Remember that crystals can break easily so avoid touching them with pliers when linking jumprings or findings.

STEP 1

Lay out your beads and all materials. Make your own eye pins using 28-gauge silver plate wire. To make an eye pin cut a length to fit easily through your beads with a short 1/4" extension either side. Make a 90° bend in the wire at one end, 1/4" in from the cut edge, using chain nose pliers. Grip the end of the wire in the jaws of round nose pliers and roll the wire in making a neat circle. Thread on your beads or motifs then make a similar eye on the other end.

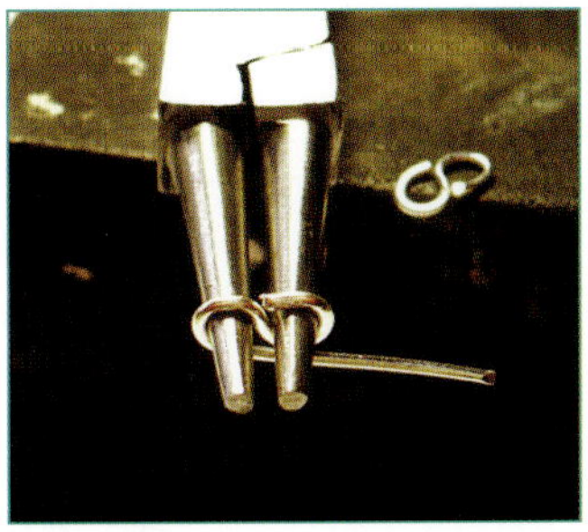

STEP 2

Make six S-shaped links using the jaws of the round nose pliers. Work straight from the roll of 1mm half-hard silver wire. Grip the cut end in the middle of the jaws of round nose pliers. Roll the wire away from you, forming a circle. Release the circle and place it on the lower jaw. Roll the wire in the opposite direction forming an S-shape. Snip off the wire with side cutters close to the center of the jaws where the wire touches the center of the S. Finish forming the link using chain nose pliers.

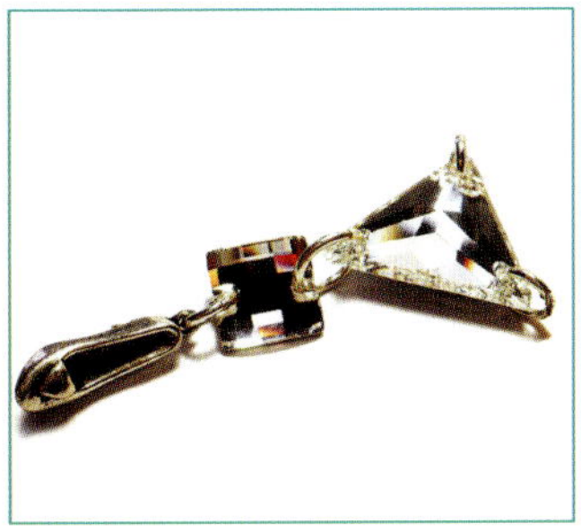

STEP 3

Place the mirror backed triangular crystal on a flat surface with the point facing the square crystal and the shoe immediately below it. Open four 6mm wide jumprings. Link a jumpring to either side of the triangular focal, but do not close them as these rings will also link to either side of the lower beaded links of the necklace. Join the square crystal to the point of the triangle with a jumpring and then the shoe to the base of the square. Close these two jumprings securely.

STEP 4

Make up the lower and upper stands of links by mixing beads and motifs to suit your individual taste. The lower stand linked to the crystal has (either side) two pearl and beaded eyepins joined together with 4mm jumprings. These are then connected to 1 1/2" lengths of chain linked to 4mm jumprings. The upper strand has a black and white bead as focal. To each side of this bead are decorated eyepins featuring pearls, silver spacers and motifs. These links are joined with the S-shaped links.

PHOTOGRAPHS: LAUREL GUILFOYLE, JOAN GORDON

STEP 5

Lay both strands of decorated links out on a flat surface as they will hang when attached to the round toggle links. The round links are the female links of toggle clasps. They join the two strands either side to the connecting chain that finishes the piece. The upper strand S-link is attached to a 6mm jumpring that in turn is linked to the toggle. The lower strand, which finishes with a chain link attached to a 4mm jumpring, is then linked to a 6mm jumpring, which connects onto the toggle. Link both sides up to form the drape of the main necklace.

STEP 6

To finish the necklace, attach a 6mm jumpring to the small round link on the end of the round toggle. Open the jumpring and link one end of the 9" length of silver chain. Close the jumpring securely and then link the opposite side of the necklace to the free end of chain in the same manner. Split the chain in equal halves with side cutters. To one end of the chain add a jumpring attached to a parrot clasp and to the other, a jumpring linked to a split ring. Take a polishing cloth and clean the surfaces of the crystals, links and chain.

Extra Projects Make earrings and a bag charm

EARRINGS

Create a simple pair of earrings by threading a silver spacer bead followed by a pearl onto an eye pin. Attach a 4mm jumpring to the base of the eyepin and link this to a crystal star drop. Link the top of the eyepin to another 4mm jumpring and link this to a fishhook earwire.

BAG CHARM

For a statement bag charm link a large crystal drop with a jumpring to a round silver disc. Link the top of the disc to a length of chain and finish with a parrot clasp.

FOCAL PENDANT

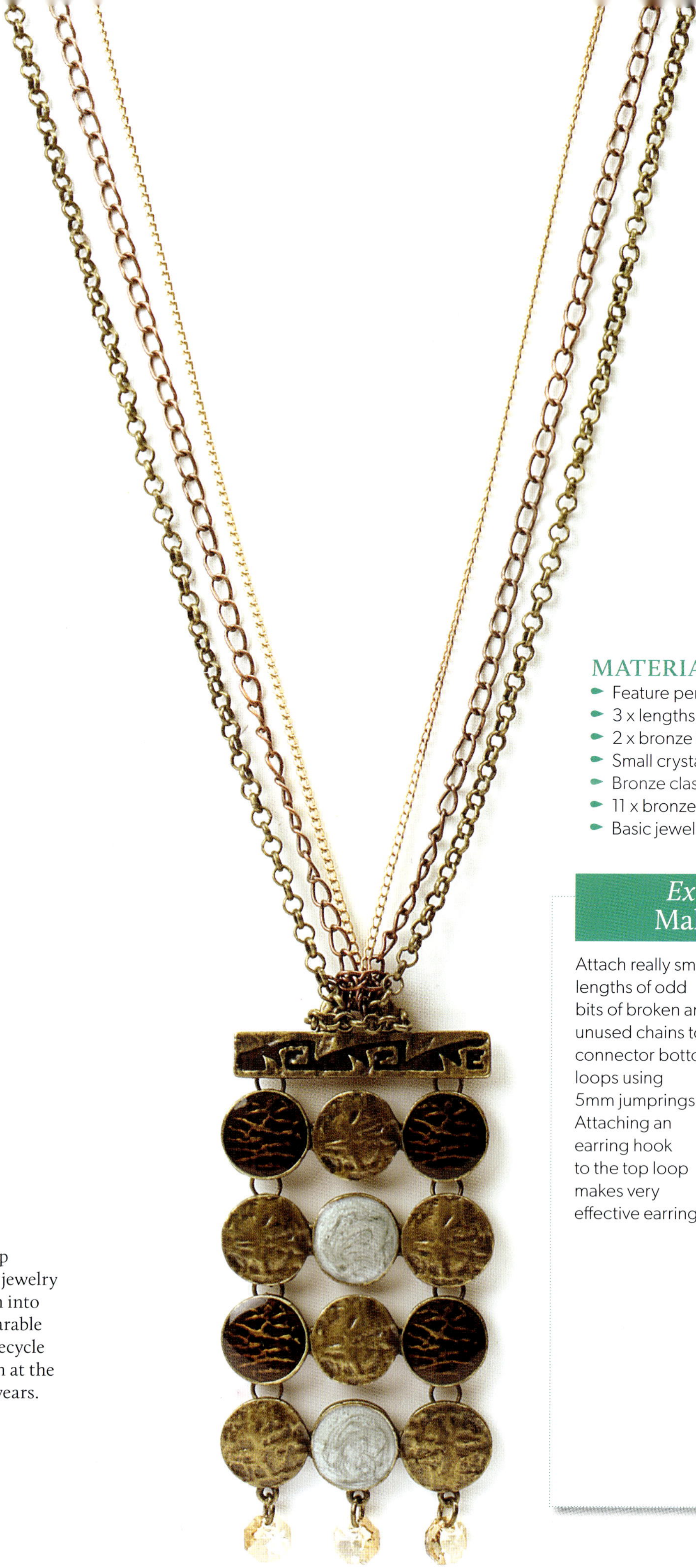

By Tansy Wilson

Upcycling! Using up pieces of unworn jewelry and turning them into something funky and wearable again is a perfect way to recycle old baubles that have been at the back of the cupboard for years.

MATERIALS

- Feature pendant (see Step 1)
- 3 x lengths of different chain
- 2 x bronze 3-strand connectors
- Small crystals, beads or charms
- Bronze clasp
- 11 x bronze 5mm jumprings
- Basic jewelry tools

Extra project Make earrings

Attach really small lengths of odd bits of broken and unused chains to connector bottom loops using 5mm jumprings. Attaching an earring hook to the top loop makes very effective earrings.

PHOTOGRAPHS: LAUREL GUILFOYLE, TANSY WHEELER

STEP 1

Sort out all your broken pieces of jewelry and see what you have to turn into another piece. You will also probably have plenty of leftover bits and bobs from other makes. Decide on what piece to have as the focal point. Look for an item that has a loop at the top.

STEP 2

Take different pieces of leftover chain and cut them all to the same length. This necklace uses long pieces of chain, but this would look equally stunning as a short necklace. Hold them all together and fold in half, passing the loop at the halfway point through the loop at the top of your pendant.

STEP 3

Pass the ends of all three chains back through the loop and pull, so the chains become fastened to the pendant. You can also try Step 2 and 3 by attaching each chain separately to obtain a slightly different look.

STEP 4

This pendant had loops on the bottom, so little crystals were attached to each one using bronze-coloured 5mm jumprings. You can also use up any leftover beads or charms here instead.

STEP 5

The only items bought for this project were these 3-loop connectors, which kept the chains separate and added a beautiful detail. If you use such connectors, add each chain using another 5mm jumpring.

STEP 6

Finally, add a clasp using more 5mm jumprings. This clasp is from another necklace and I loved it so much I couldn't throw it away. I am so glad it's back on a piece!

Designer tips

- If you don't have chains available you could also use ribbons, leather or lace to obtain a different look.
- The possibilities for creating jewellery are endless and you can be creative in mixing up different elements.

SEEDBEAD STYLE

By Tansy Wilson

This bracelet is a simple jumpring linked chain. It's really easy to make and you can add in any color of seed bead. Just make sure your beads are big enough to fit on the jumprings.

MATERIALS

- 35 x gold 6mm jumprings
- 35 x 3mm red glass foil-lined beads
- 35 x 3mm green glass foil-lined beads
- Gold toggle clasp
- Basic jewelry tools

Designer tip

- It's a good idea to invest in a pair of chain nose pliers for this sort of beading and linking. The design of the nose of the pliers means you can see what you are doing.

STEP 1

Check that your beads have a large enough hole to fit onto your jumprings. This bracelet uses 3mm glass foil-lined beads and a 6mm jumpring.

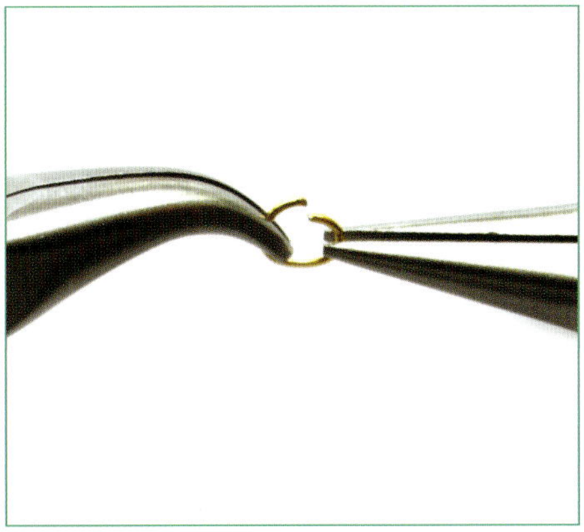

STEP 2

Open a jumpring by holding it between two pairs of pliers. Turn your left hand away from you and your right hand towards you, twisting the jumpring rather than pulling the join apart.

PHOTOGRAPHS: LAUREL GUILFOYLE, TANSY WHEELER

STEP 3

Twist it open enough to thread a red and a green glass bead onto it. Twist the jumpring back again to close it up.

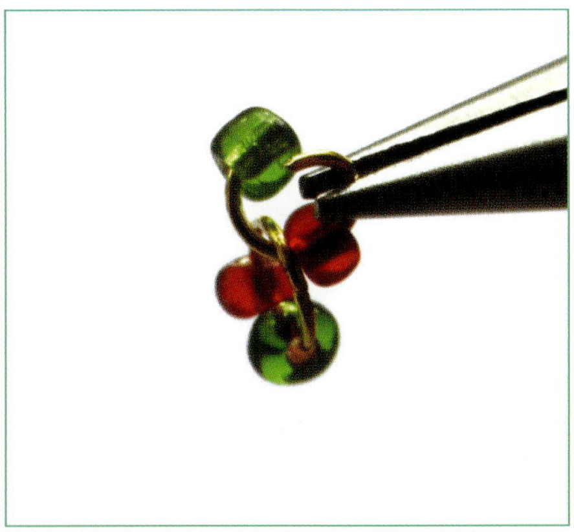

STEP 4

Twist open another jumpring and thread on one red bead. Then link the jumpring through the beaded ring, completed in Step 3, before threading on a green bead. Twist the jumpring closed, joining them together.

STEP 5

Repeat Steps 2 to 4 so you are linking the beaded jumprings together. I have alternated my colored beads but this isn't necessary, as the bracelet will twist around on your wrist.

STEP 6

An average adult wrist length is approx. 7". When you have reached your desired length, before closing the last jumpring at each end, add a toggle clasp to one and a toggle bar to the other.

Extra project Make a necklace

This would be a perfect piece for a winter cruise or holiday. Use 4mm mock turquoise Howlite beads and 6mm jumprings to make the necklace. It is long enough not to require a clasp and just slips over your head. Just join the last jumpring to the first one added at the other end.

MILLEFIORI SQUARES

By Tansy Wilson

The inspiration for this bracelet came from using Italian millefiore beads, which translated means a thousand flowers. This distinctive glass technique has been around since the 1840s and is incredibly beautiful.

MATERIALS

- 3 x 30mm x 30mm glass millefiore beads
- 2 x 30mm x 30mm silver square connectors
- 0.8mm (20 gauge) silver colored wire – to make your own eye pins
- 1 x square toggle clasp
- 20 x 4mm jumprings
- Basic jewelry tools

Extra Projects Make a pendant and earrings

The glass millefiore beads come on a strand of mixed colors. This means you can make matching items like this fabulous pendant or earrings. Simply thread a headpin through the glass square bead and form an eyeloop at the other side. Then using two 4mm jumprings, link to earring hooks or a pendant bail.

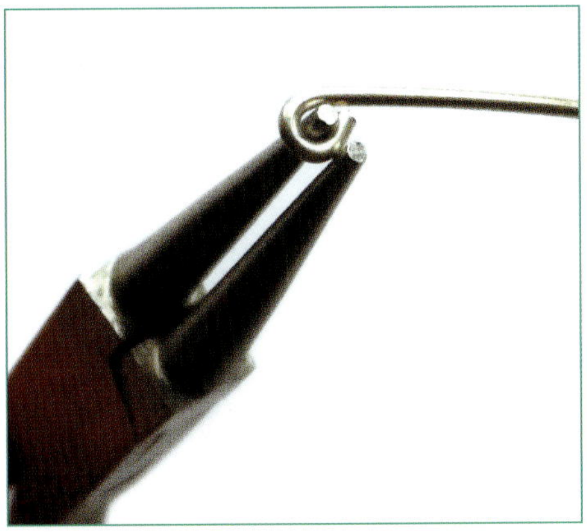

STEP 1

When using such large beads, it's easier to make your own eye pins. Hold the very end of the wire between the jaws on round nose pliers. The nearer the tip of the jaws the smaller the loop you will make. Bend the wire to form a circle.

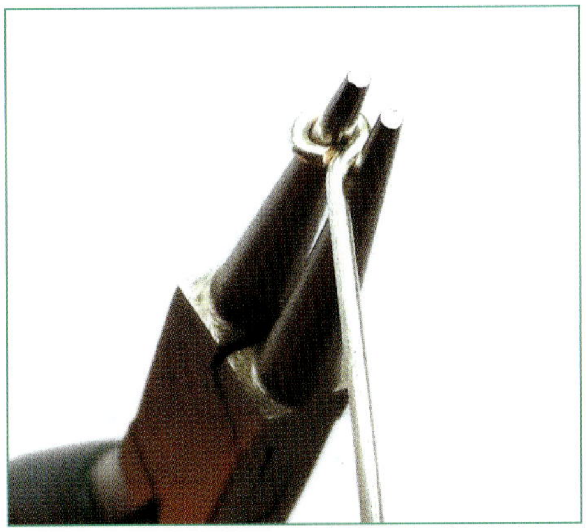

STEP 2

Remove the wire from the jaws and reposition the pliers so they are now gripping the outside of the wire opposite the beginning of the circle. You can then bend the long length of wire against the jaws to form the stem of the eye pin.

STEP 3

Push the eye pin through the large square glass bead so the eye is tight against the bead. Then bend the pin poking out the other side at an angle directly against the bead. Bend it in the same direction as the eyeloop on the other side.

STEP 4

Grip the wire in your round nose pliers at the same place on the jaws, as in Step 1, so you will create the same size hole. Holding the long length of wire in your fingers, wrap it around the jaws to create another circle of wire. Cut away the excess. Repeat Steps 1–4 to add eye pins to all your glass beads.

STEP 5

Using 4mm jumprings, open one and link it through the loop on your eye pin and the hole on the square connector and then close. Repeat this step using another jumpring. Repeat to join all the glass beads and square connectors together.

STEP 6

Finally you need to add the toggle clasp to each end again using two jumprings. You can keep adding pairs of jumprings to obtain the correct wrist measurement.

PHOTOGRAPHS: LAUREL GUILFOYLE, TANSY WHEELER

BOLLYWOOD

By Tansy Wilson

The main inspiration behind these earrings is the glamour of Bollywood combined with the beautiful colors and ornate architecture of Indian temples. The pretty delicate seed bead flowers work well against the traditional gold and elaborate structure of the earrings, making them just perfect for any rising star.

MATERIALS

- 24 x gold-colored half circle connectors
- 36 x 4mm gold-colored jumprings
- 2 x gold-colored earring hooks
- 20 x 4mm gold-colored round beads
- 60 x turquoise seed beads
- 10 x 4mm coral beads
- Beading thread and needle
- Basic jewelry tools

Extra Project Variation on design

Following Steps 1–4, make the bead flowers using bicone crystals. This creates a completely different effect. Use 4mm for the five central beads and 6mm for the five outer petals with the same seed beads as used in the main project. Thread straight onto an earring hook for a subtler look.

STEP 1

Cut approximately 12" from a roll of beading thread and thread through the eye of a beading needle. Pick up five turquoise seed beads and center them on the thread. Then thread the beading needle back through all five beads and pull the ends so they start to form a circle.

STEP 2

To completely tighten the circle, pass the beading needle back through the very first bead you initially picked up. Ensure you pass the needle the opposite way to the direction that the thread is already coming out. When you then pull the two ends all the beads will fit together to make a flower shape.

STEP 3

Pick up a 4mm gold bead followed by another turquoise seed bead. Thread the needle back through the gold bead only. Pull the beads so they move close to the flower shape and you will be able to thread the beading needle through the hole of the nearest seed bead from the flower. When you pull tightly the gold bead nestles in between these two beads.

PHOTOGRAPHS: LAUREL GUILFOYLE, TANSY WHEELER

STEP 4

Keep repeating Step 3 so you add three more gold beads. When you add the final gold and seed bead, before threading back through the gold bead, add a jumpring. Pull the threads and you will see that you have worked your way round to meet where you started. Tie a knot and thread back through a few beads before cutting away excess. This will prevent the knots unravelling through wear. Repeat Steps 1–4 to make six flower dangles.

STEP 5

Open a jumpring and link two of your half circle connectors together and keep repeating so you create the formation as illustrated in the picture above. Note that two jumprings hold the bottom half circle.

STEP 6

Continue to open jumprings and link on the rest of the half circle connectors to resemble the pattern as shown above. Note that the three middle circles do not connect. Repeat Steps 5–6 for the other base shape. Open the jumprings on the tops of the flower dangles and add to the top, middle and bottom of the diamond shaped forms. Finally add an earring hook to each one.

BASIC TECHNIQUES

HOW TO MAKE A WRAPPED LOOP

1. Thread a bead onto a headpin or eye pin. Grip the wire with round nose pliers next to the bead.

2. Bend the wire above the plier jaw to a right angle. You will need about $^{1}/_{8}$" of wire above the bead before the bend.

3. Move the plier jaws to sit at the top of the bend.

4. With your thumb push the wire back around the pliers, keeping it tight to the jaw.

5. Keep pushing the wire around the jaw until you meet the bead.

6. Move the pliers around the loop and continue to bend the wire around until it is facing out at a right angle and you have a complete loop.

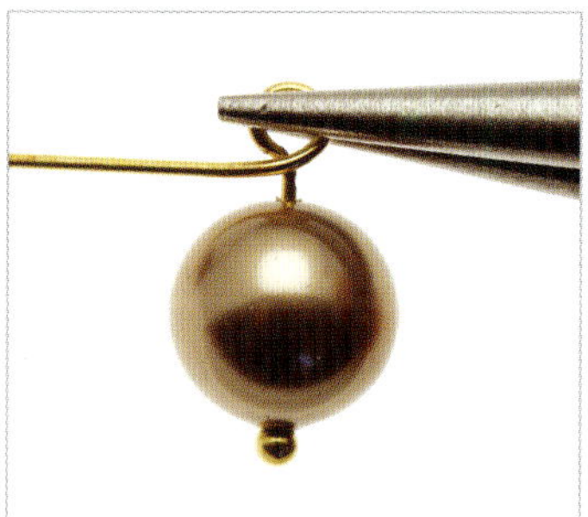

7. If attaching the loop to a chain this is the stage to do that. Use a pair of chain nose pliers to hold across the loop firmly.

8. Wrap the wire around the neck of the loop until it meets the bead. Snip off any excess wire and push the end against the coil to finish.

MAKING A SIMPLE LOOP

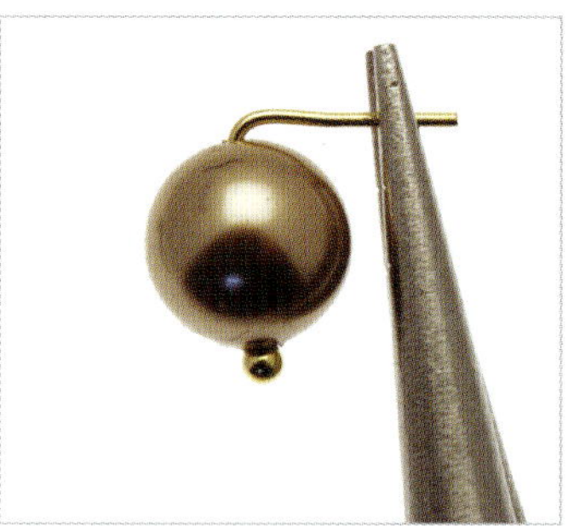

1. Thread the bead onto a headpin or eye pin and cut the pin about $^{3}/_{8}$" above the bead. Bend the wire to a right angle above the bead.

2. Using round nose pliers, grasp the wire at the very end and curl it around the plier jaws.

3. Roll the wire around to meet the bead. Bend the loop back to sit directly above the bead.

4. Use chain nose pliers to tighten the loop by twisting it from side to side. Do not pull it outwards as that will distort the shape.

PHOTOGRAPHS: SIAN HAMILTON

USING JUMPRINGS

Always make sure you follow this guide and don't pull jumprings apart as they can easily distort.

Take a jumpring in two pairs of pliers with the opening centered at the top.

Hold the jumpring either as shown in the step above or this step.

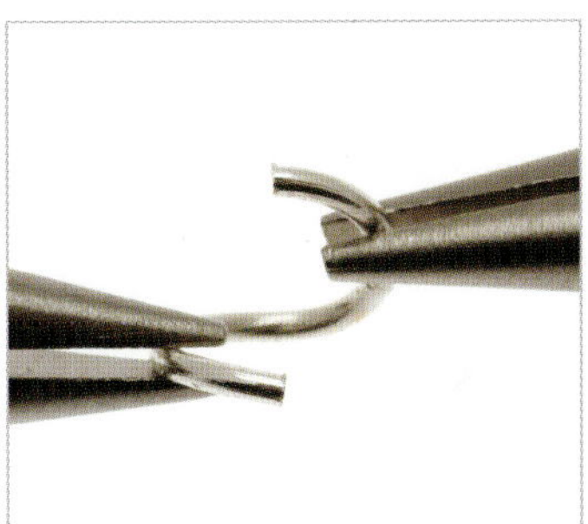

Whichever way you hold the jumpring, the opening motion is the same. Twist one hand towards you and the other hand away; never pull apart. Reverse the action to close.

CRIMPING A BEAD

To show this process clearly it is being shown without using thread; the thread or wire should be inside the bead.

Hold the crimp bead in the pliers with the bead in the hole that has a round side opposite a 'W' shape.

Before closing the pliers, check that the bead is straight. When you close the pliers the thread or wire should fall either side of the bend.

Move the 'U' shape crimp to the other hole with two round sides. Turn the crimp so the 'U' faces sideways and press the pliers closed tightly.

ADDING A COVER

Crimp covers make your finished jewelry look more professional and clean.

Take a crimp cover and place it over the crimped bead, making sure the bead is completely inside the cover.

Take a pair of chain or flat nose pliers and carefully grasp the cover. Gently press the cover closed.

The finished bead should be closed into a perfect bead shape. Nylon nose pliers do this job very well as they won't mark the cover.

MAKING AN EYE PIN

Make your own eye pins using 0.8mm (or 0.7mm) wire. You can use 1mm if you need strong pins.

Take the very end of the wire in round nose pliers. If the wire is quite hard it may slip out of the pliers, so start the loop about 1/8" in and snip off the straight piece as you make the first curve.

The shape you want to create is a P. The advantage to making your own eyepins is that you can make the loop any size you need.

To finish the pin so the loop sits centered on the wire, take the round nose pliers and place them where the round P shape meets the wire. Press the wire back against the pliers until the loop is centered.

BASIC TOOLS

TYPES OF PLIERS

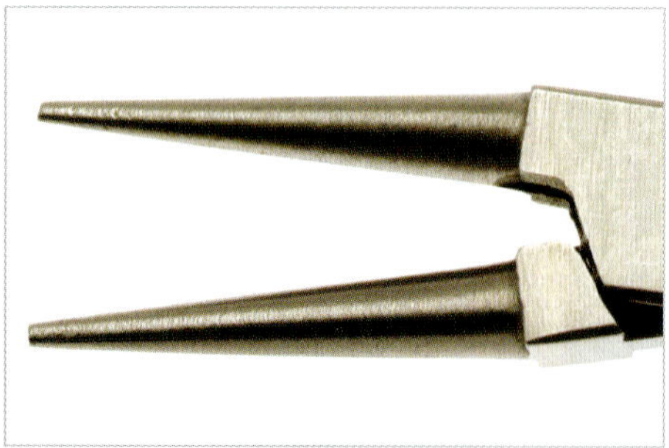

ROUND NOSE

These are a must-have for a basic kit. When making jewelry, being able to create loops and rings is essential.

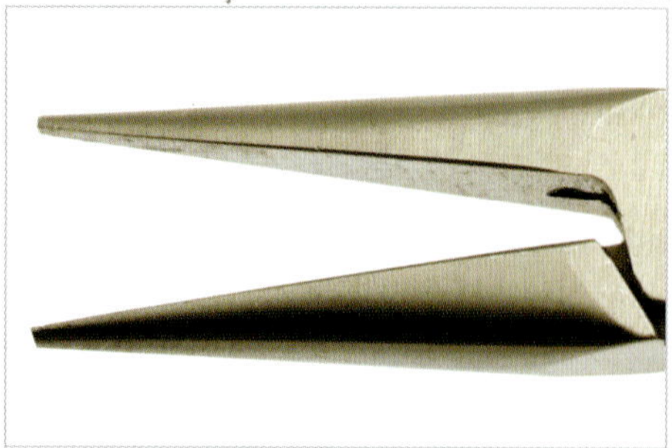

CHAIN NOSE

Also called half round, these are the most versatile. They are used for many jewelry applications, so are another must-have for the basic kit.

FLAT NOSE

Similar to chain nose, these pliers have a wider jaw that is completely flat. Good for holding jumprings/findings as the wide jaw grasps a large area.

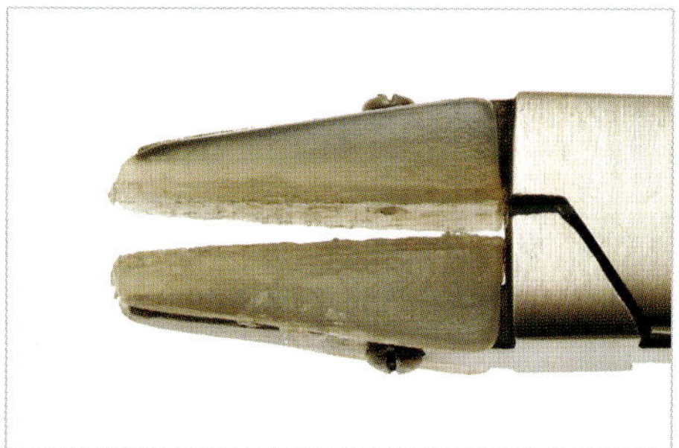

NYLON NOSE

Another similar style to flat nose, these pliers have jaws that are covered in nylon to stop them marking the metal.

BENT NOSE

Used for getting into small tricky spaces where a straight nose pair cannot reach.

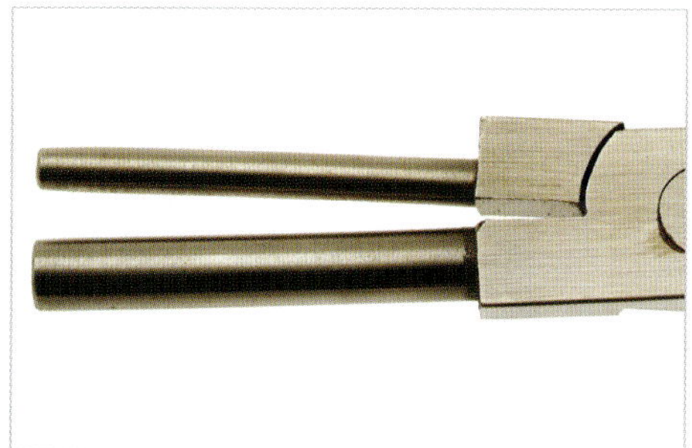

BAIL MAKING

These pliers have fixed sized jaws, with each jaw being a different size, usually with a 2mm difference (such as 3mm and 5mm). They come in a wide variety of sizes and are great if making a lot of the same size jumprings or coils.

CRIMPING

These pliers are used with crimp beads. If you want to have a nice finish to your crimping then these pliers are a good investment.

CUTTERS/SNIPS

These pliers are also called side cutters. They come in a vast range of prices and styles. Be careful what you cut as they can blunt easily if used with hard or large dimension wire.

MEMORY CUTTERS

Used exclusively for cutting memory wire. If you are going to use memory wire you must invest in these; the wire will damage standard cutters.